THE NATION'S
REPORT
CARD

Learning to Be Literate in America

Reading, Writing, and Reasoning

Arthur N. Applebee
Judith A. Langer
Ina V. S. Mullis

March 1987

Table of Contents

This report is based primarily on the following NAEP reports:

The Reading Report Card, Progress Toward Excellence in Our Schools, Trends in Reading over Four National Assessments, 1971-1984. National Assessment of Educational Progress, Educational Testing Service, 1985.

A. Applebee, J. Langer, and I. Mullis. *Writing Trends Across the Decade, 1974-84*. National Assessment of Educational Progress, Educational Testing Service, 1986.

I. Kirsch and A. Jungeblut. *Literacy: Profiles of America's Young Adults*. National Assessment of Educational Progress, Educational Testing Service, 1986.

A. Applebee, J. Langer, and I. Mullis. *The Writing Report Card, Writing Achievement in American Schools*. National Assessment of Educational Progress, Educational Testing Service, 1986.

These reports are available from NAEP, CN 6710, Princeton, NJ 08541-6710. *The Reading Report Card* is $9.00, *Writing Trends Across the Decade, 1974-84* is $12.50, *Literacy: Profiles of America's Young Adults* is $12.50, *The Writing Report Card* is $12.50; orders require $1.50 for shipping and handling.

Foreword

Literacy in its most basic form is simply the ability to read and write. This report is about literacy in America. It's about how well most of the children and young adults in this country can read simple texts and how well they can express simple ideas in writing.

The good news is that virtually all of our children and young adults are basically literate. The bad news is that minimum levels of literacy are no longer sufficient for people who must live and work in an increasingly complex and technological society.

According to the National Assessment of Educational Progress, only a small percentage of the young people sampled in its recent studies can reason effectively about what they read and write. That means that the majority don't have the critical thinking skills we need in an economy like ours that's based on information and knowledge. The office, not the factory, is the center of our working lives. The backbone of the new American work force will be people who deal mainly with the formation and the refinement of ideas.

Literacy—real literacy—is the essential raw material of the information age. We are entering an era of lifelong learning that merges work and education. Most jobs of the future will be restructured at least once every seven years. By 1990, three out of four jobs will require some education or technical training after high school.

American business needs workers who not only are proficient in the basic skills, but who know how to think and can communicate what they're thinking. We need workers who can adjust to change, who can absorb new ideas and share them easily with others. In short, we need people who have learned how to learn.

And yet, our high schools graduate 700,000 functionally illiterate young people every year—and another 700,000 drop out. According to Secretary of Labor William E. Brock, it is an "insane national tragedy" that 700,000 high school graduates get diplomas each year and cannot read them.

In 16 states, dropout rates range from 26 percent to 42 percent, and most big cities are at the high end of that. What's worse, most of those who do stay in school don't learn enough to meet even minimum academic standards.

Today, nine out of 10 colleges offer noncredit remedial courses in English and math to their incoming freshmen. The U.S. Department of Education says that as many as three out of five high school graduates who enter college require remedial work.

If current demographic and economic trends continue, American business will have to hire a million new workers a year who can't read, write or count. Teaching them how, and absorbing the lost productivity while they're learning, will cost industry $25 billion a year for as long as it takes—and nobody seems to know how long that will be.

One out of three major corporations already gives new workers basic reading, writing, and arithmetic courses. Corporations spend $210 billion a year on training, and one percent of that—roughly $2 billion a year—now goes to teaching basic skills.

The problem is not limited to the private sector. Most government agencies provide high school level courses in reading, writing, grammar and vocabulary. In 1984, for example, the U.S. Army spent more than $14 million to bring its new recruits up to the ninth grade level in reading—and 90 percent of them were high school graduates.

Clearly, we have to rethink our education system from the ground up. Reform and reorganization are desperately needed. But they are long-term goals that could take an entire generation to achieve, and I don't think we have that much time.

Secretary Brock has said that there will be a job in the future for every qualified person who wants one. The real question, he warns, is: Are we going to have enough qualified persons to fill those jobs?

NAEP reminds us that as a nation we can be proud of the literacy levels we've attained, but "it is crucial that we do better."

Unfortunately, this report confirms what many of us in business have known for some time. The basic skills of our entry-level workers are simply not good enough to give us the kind of work force we need to compete in a fiercely competitive global market. This is no less than a survival issue for America.

David T. Kearns
Chairman and Chief Executive Officer
Xerox Corporation

Learning to Be Literate in America

The recent Nation's Report Cards based on NAEP assessments of reading, writing, and literacy indicate that most children and young adults can understand what they read and can express their thoughts in writing at a surface level. Only a small percentage, however, can reason effectively about what they are reading or writing. The NAEP data also suggest that there are serious disparities in literacy learning among American schoolchildren. Black children, Hispanic children, children living in disadvantaged urban communities, and those whose parents have low levels of education are particularly at risk for future educational failure. In spite of gains during the past decade, the performance of these groups remains far below national averages.

The results suggest two important initiatives that should concern us—as educators, as policymakers, and as a nation:

■ We must provide targeted help for the at-risk populations to ensure that everyone has the opportunity to develop the varied literacy skills necessary for full and effective participation in our society.

■ We must modify our approaches to education so that all children learn to reason more effectively about what they read and write, giving them the thinking skills to analyze, elaborate upon, and extend the ideas with which they are dealing.

Introduction

Literacy—the ability to read and write, and to reason effectively about what one reads or writes—is an integral part of life and work in the United States. The literacy of the work force is a resource for business and industry; the literacy of schoolchildren is an indicator of the success of our schools; the literacy of our citizens is important in the functioning of our democratic processes of government. We expect that our populace will learn to read and write, and society is structured around its ability to do so. In comparison with those who are more literate, individuals who lack such skills have fewer opportunities open to them in all aspects of their lives.

Yet, particularly in recent years, the role of literacy in American society has changed. The technological and information systems available to individuals at both home and work have accentuated the differences in opportunities available to those who have well-developed literacy skills and those who do not. On the one hand, technology is reducing the literacy skills needed to complete routine tasks; on the other hand, the skills needed to develop and control these technologies are becoming increasingly complex. While the needs of the work force do not require that all individuals have advanced literacy skills, the lack of such skills can prevent them from attaining positions that they may desire.

Society has also grown more complex, offering more opportunities and presenting more choices in its economic, political, and social systems. People are constantly confronted with new decisions to make as well as with new things to learn about—and written information usually guides their choices. (This is true even when the written word is then presented orally, as in radio and television reports and commercials.) Changes in society have created the need for new levels of literacy, and have exacerbated the differences in the opportunities available to those who are literate and those who are not. These changes in society have affected the lives of all of us.

Our everyday uses of literacy are sometimes more abstract—and sometimes more complex—than in the past. And because these changes have permeated society, they have made an appreciable difference both in the ways in which we think about literacy and in what and how we teach in our schools.

Though the importance of literacy is universally acknowledged, there is much less agreement about what it means to be literate. There are many different taxonomies used to specify the skills involved in reading and writing, as well as many definitions of what literacy means. Our discussions will focus on two important components of literacy: 1) the ability to derive **surface understanding** from written materials and to express similar understanding in writing; and 2) the ability to **reason effectively** about what one reads and writes in order to extend one's understanding of the ideas expressed. For us, these abilities mark the fully literate person in today's society.

The Ability to Understand at a Surface Level

Surface understanding of written materials is a necessary component of literacy, though it is not always sufficient. In school and in society, people engage in a wide array of reading and writing activities requiring surface-level understanding. Some of these tasks require only simple skills because the material is very familiar or the goals of the activity are uncomplicated. Other tasks require broader and more varied skills. Making sense of a shopping list requires different skills from those required to understand a letter from a friend, and these skills differ from those needed for a surface understanding of a report of a recently completed science experiment. Similarly, writing one's own shopping list requires somewhat different skills from writing a letter to a friend, and these differ in turn from those needed to write one's own report of a science experiment.

Literacy activities that call only for surface understanding take place frequently at home, school, and work. Such understanding is also part of thinking more carefully about what one is reading or writing. Therefore, in becoming increasingly literate, schoolchildren must develop the ability to understand a variety of increasingly more difficult materials at least at a surface level.

The Ability to Reason Effectively about One's Reading and Writing

Although surface understanding is important, it is not enough. In school and in society, we expect a reader to be able to analyze, evaluate, and extend the ideas that are presented, just as we expect a writer to elaborate upon and defend judgments that are expressed. We expect people to know how to get information and to know how to use it and shape it to suit their needs. For example, readers must learn to relate what they are reading to their personal experience in order to integrate new ideas with what they know — perhaps modifying or rejecting the ideas in the process of considering them more fully. Readers must also learn to test the validity of what they read by comparing it with information from other sources, as well as to judge the internal logic and consistency of the ideas and information presented.

Similar thinking abilities are important in writing. To develop their surface understanding and convey their ideas to others, writers must learn to draw upon their personal experiences, to incorporate information from other sources, and to evaluate the internal consistency and organization of their ideas and arguments.

Such systematic reasoning about what they read and write gives literate people the kinds of mastery of the written word required by more and more activities in today's society. To gain such mastery, children must have the opportunity to develop their abilities to reason effectively in the variety of situations in which reading and writing are used.

The Nation's Report Card: National Assessment of Educational Progress

In examining the state of literacy, we will be drawing on a series of recent assessments carried out by NAEP. These assessments examined the reading and writing achievement of school-age children, as well as the literacy skills of young adults, ages 21 through 25. The NAEP results provide a solid base for examining both the overall state of literacy and the many factors that influence adult literacy levels and the success of our schools.* They offer a more extensive portrait of the reading and writing achievement of the nation's children and young adults than has previously been available. This provides us with a unique basis for presenting this overview of literacy development in America and offering suggestions for improving literacy education.

*Detailed results from these assessments are available in a series of reports from NAEP: *The Reading Report Card*, *Writing Trends Across the Decade*, *The Writing Report Card*, and *Literacy: Profiles of America's Young Adults*.

Chapter 2

The State of Literacy in America

The results across a variety of assessments present a consistent picture of the state of literacy in America:

■ **Most** children and young adults demonstrate a **surface understanding** of a range of materials appropriate for their age.

■ Only **small percentages** of children and young adults can **reason effectively** about what they are reading or writing.

In fostering literacy in America, we have made an impressive beginning—but not enough people are developing the advanced literacy skills that are needed in our increasingly complex and technological society.

Schooling and Literacy Skills

Are students learning to read and write better as they move through school?

At one level, the results are encouraging: They reflect a steady growth in performance in both reading and writing across the age groups assessed. To compare performance across groups, NAEP derived a reading-proficiency scale ranging from 0 to 500, and a writing-achievement scale ranging from 0 to 400. Results from the scales are shown in **Figure 2.1**. Changes in mean performance reflect an increase in literacy skills from one age group to another. For reading proficiency, performance levels increased from a mean of 218 at grade 4 to a mean of 305 in the young adult samples. Writing achievement shows corresponding increases, rising from an initial level of 158 in grade 4 to 219 in grade 11.

These results suggest that schools do make a difference in literacy skills; the

Figure 2.1. **Average Reading and Writing Levels for the Nation**

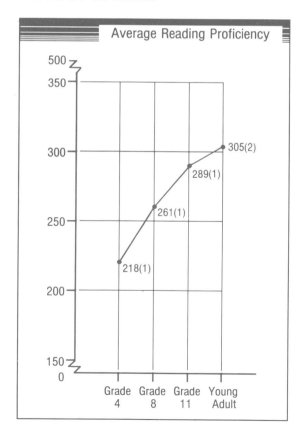

more schooling students receive, the more literate they are likely to become.

This interpretation is reinforced if we consider the relationship between reading proficiency levels and amount of education in the young adult sample. Young adults who did not complete high school actually read about the same as eighth grade students in the national sample (averaging 263 on the reading proficiency scale compared with 261 for eighth graders), while those

The estimated population means are presented with their standard errors shown in parentheses. It can be said with 95 percent certainty that the mean reading or writing level of the population of interest is within the interval ±2 standard errors. Means and standard errors have been rounded.

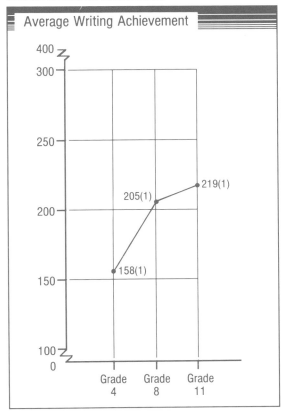

Average Writing Achievement

with college degrees did much better than the young adult sample as a whole (averaging 336 compared with 305 for the sample as a whole).

To understand what these levels mean, we need to examine the kinds of performance the scales reflect.

Levels of Reading Proficiency

Higher levels on the reading scale reflect both the ability to understand more difficult material at a surface level and the ability to think critically and purposefully about what the material says.

Reading tasks at the basic level (200) tap the ability to derive a surface understanding from relatively simple material, such as brief newspaper articles or stories. Tasks at the adept level and above (over 300) present the reader with more difficult texts, more difficult questions, or less familiar subject matter. To deal with these tasks, readers need the ability to draw on a range of reasoning skills in order to make sense of what they encounter. The intermediate level (250) is a transitional level, reflecting successful performance on relatively longer but still quite straightforward literacy tasks.

How well do the nation's young people read?

Results from recent reading assessments of schoolchildren and young adults are summarized in **Table 2.1**. At fourth grade, nearly all students (96 percent) had at least rudimentary reading skills, and the majority (68 percent) had the basic comprehension skills necessary to locate information in simple reading materials. **Some 97 percent of the young adults had attained basic comprehension skills, and 84 percent had attained intermediate levels.**

Performance at these levels suggests the ability to derive a surface understanding from a variety of texts, locating information and making simple generalizations about what is read.

Performance at higher levels on the reading scale, however, was much more limited. Only about half of the young adults assessed could be classified as adept readers, able to deal relatively well with complicated literary and informational material such as might be encountered in a high-school text. On tasks measuring the advanced reading skills needed to deal with specialized and complex texts similar to those found in college, professional, and technical working environments, only one fifth of the young adults

Table 2.1 **Percentage of Students and Young Adults At or Above Five Reading Proficiency Levels***

Reading Skills and Strategies	Grade 4	Grade 8	Grade 11	Young Adults
Advanced (350): Synthesize and learn from specialized reading materials.	0%	0%	5%	21%
Adept (300): Find, understand, summarize, and explain relatively complicated information.	1	13	40	54
Intermediate (250): Search for specific information, interrelate ideas, and make generalizations.	20	63	85	84
Basic (200): Understand specific or sequentially related materials.	68	96	99	97
Rudimentary (150): Carry out simple, discrete reading tasks.	96	100	100	100

*Age level (rather than grade level) data for 9-, 13-, and 17-year-olds are presented in *The Reading Report Card*.

were successful. Such tasks require the ability to reason effectively about what is read—and few people were able to do so.

Levels of Writing Achievement

Like the reading scale, better performance on the writing scale reflects both the ability to express one's surface understanding of increasingly complex ideas and situations and the ability to think these ideas through more thoroughly while writing about them.* For individual writing items, responses that demonstrated an understanding of some of the elements necessary to accomplish the task (but not an ability to use them well enough to accomplish the purpose of writing) were scored as minimal (200); those that included sufficient information to accomplish the task were scored as adequate (300), though they did not necessarily show much grace or polish. Responses at the 400 level reflect the ability to present fully elaborated ideas in a particularly well-organized manner, with supporting detail that is appropriate to the particular task— in other words, the ability to develop one's thoughts logically and effectively in writing.

How well do the nation's students write?

In the writing assessment, students responded at least at a minimal or surface level to a range of writing tasks appropriate to their grade level. For example, on simple tasks as many as 90 percent of the eleventh graders responded at least at the minimal level, while even on the most difficult task 60 percent responded at this level.

---

*Due to the different analytic procedures used to create the writing scale, a table reporting writing performance comparable to Table 2.1 for reading could not be generated (see *The Writing Report Card*).

Far fewer of the responses, however, reflected the ability to reason effectively about what was being written. Performance at the adequate level was distressingly rare, even on simple tasks that required little thinking through. For example, only 65 percent of the eleventh graders could write an adequate paragraph on a job application describing the kind of job they would like, only 67 percent of the eighth graders could write a letter of complaint to a T-shirt company and suggest a course of action to remedy their problem, and only 41 percent of the fourth graders could describe information presented in a brief series of simple pictures. These tasks required the students to write about information they already knew (or could easily understand) in a straightforward manner.

When the tasks became more complex, requiring more extended reasoning in order to plan and carry out the writing, only small percentages of students at any grade were able to perform adequately. For example, in response to a task requiring them to write a letter persuading the school principal to drop an unnecessary school rule, only 22 percent of the eleventh graders, 15 percent of the eighth graders, and 4 percent of the fourth graders wrote at the adequate level or better. Tasks that required the students to write reasoned papers for a particular purpose were difficult for students of all ages to complete successfully.

In general, American students have learned the fundamentals of writing. There is a steady increase in writing ability across the grades, and most students write with the surface understanding and skill needed for a minimal level of writing performance on tasks appropriate to their grade level.

The data suggest, however, that a substantial proportion of eleventh graders, who are almost ready to graduate from high school and enter higher education or the job market, will not be able to write adequately enough to serve their own needs. Their writing does not reflect the kinds of writing performance required for success in school or at work. They have not developed the effective reasoning skills required to adequately communicate their ideas in ways that will be understood by others.

Conclusion

Are America's children and young adults literate? To some extent they are. All but a small percentage of the nation's young people can understand what they read and can express their ideas at a surface level. But minimum literacy levels are not enough— not for successful participation in many of the school, work, community, and leisure activities in which today's Americans participate. These contexts require the ability to reason effectively about what one is reading or writing, and far too many of our young people appear to lack effective thinking skills.

The national concern about literacy performance is real, and rightly so. Business, industry, and the public have recognized that many young people have not developed the ability to reason effectively about what they read and write and are thus not able to perform many of the literacy activities they may encounter in today's technological and information society. Times have changed, and the opportunities available to our students have changed with them. Today, the ability to reason effectively about what one reads and writes should be a primary goal of American education—for all students at every age.

Chapter

Who Is At Risk?

In a nation as diverse as this, it is important to ensure that young people from all groups within the society have an equal opportunity to become literate. Data from the most recent national assessments indicate that there are two groups who are particularly at risk for school failure if they do not receive additional educational attention: children and young adults who are members of particular minority groups, and those who lack home support for literacy.

Children and Young Adults from Minority Groups

To what extent are children and young adults from at-risk minority groups within American society learning to be literate?

Certain minority groups have historically been at a disadvantage within American society. In order to examine how such groups are faring, NAEP has looked separately at the achievement of Black and Hispanic students, in comparison with their White classmates.* The relevant scores for reading and writing proficiency of children

*NAEP has limited information on the performance of Asian-American students. However, results from *The Writing Report Card* indicate that their performance is comparable to that of their White classmates.

and young adults are displayed in **Figure 3.1. At all three grade levels, Hispanic and Black students read and write far less well than their White classmates.** The differences in achievement between the two minority groups are small, though Hispanic students perform slightly better at all grades than do their Black counterparts. Hispanic young adults, on average, per-

Figure 3.1. **Average Reading and Writing Levels for Black, Hispanic, and White Students and Young Adults**

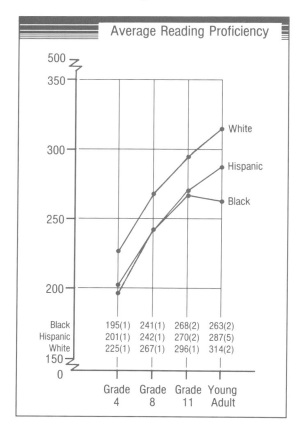

form about midway between their Black and White peers.

For the most part, young adults show higher reading performance than do eleventh-grade students. Although Black young adults, on average, do not show improved performance compared to Black in-school students at grade 11, those who

---

The estimated population means are presented with their standard errors shown in parentheses. It can be said with 95 percent certainty that the mean reading or writing level of the population of interest is within the interval ±2 standard errors. Means and standard errors have been rounded.

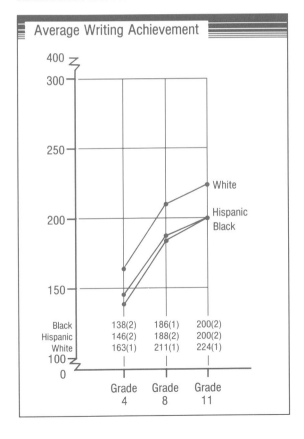

Average Writing Achievement

	Grade 4	Grade 8	Grade 11
Black	138(2)	186(1)	200(2)
Hispanic	146(2)	188(2)	200(2)
White	163(1)	211(1)	224(1)

receive postsecondary schooling read more proficiently than those who do not. Among young Black and Hispanic adults, however, even those who are college educated retain their disadvantage relative to their White age-mates.

Another way to think about the performance of these minority young adults is to compare it to the average performance of students at the three grade levels assessed by NAEP. Black young adults, on average, read slightly better than eighth-grade students nationally, and Hispanic young adults, on average, read slightly less well than eleventh-grade students nationally. The results by grade level are summarized in **Table 3.1**. Although there is a discrepancy in the performance of young adults in the two minority groups, clearly both read substantially less well than their White age-mates and are at a considerable disadvantage in situations that call for more advanced literacy skills.

It should be stressed that the distributions of performance overlap considerably for the White, Black, and Hispanic populations. Some Black and Hispanic children and young adults are among the best readers and writers, and some White children and young adults are among the nation's poorest readers and writers. However, the obvious inequities for our nation's minority students must not be ignored. **As a group, Black and Hispanic students are well behind White students by grade 4, and the difference is not made up even for those who attend college.**

Most young adults feel that their literacy skills are appropriate for their present jobs, but many Black and His-

Table 3.1 **Percent of Black, Hispanic, and White Young Adults At or Above Average 4th-, 8th-, and 11th-Grade Reading Levels on the NAEP Scale**

	Black	Hispanic	White
Grade 11 (289)	31%	52%	68%
Grade 8 (261)	53	71	85
Grade 4 (218)	82	92	96

panic young adults also recognize the importance of improving these literacy skills if they are to obtain better jobs. About 70 percent of the Black and 60 percent of the Hispanic young adults felt the need for additional reading and writing skills, in contrast with 36 percent of their White age-mates. Similarly, 79 percent of the Black and 69 percent of the Hispanic young adults expect to obtain more literacy training. Their disadvantage is real, and they recognize the need to remedy it.

To what extent have these gaps in performance been reduced during the past decade?

Results from assessments of reading proficiency between 1971 and 1984 indicate that schools have had some success in reducing disparities in performance, by improving the achievement of at-risk minority students without reducing the achievement of the majority. For example, in 1971 close to one-third of the Black children assessed at age 9 lacked even rudimentary reading skills. In 1984, this had been reduced to 16 percent. During the same period, the percentage of White

9-year-olds lacking such skills was also reduced, from 6 to 4 percent. The reading proficiency of Hispanic students was not separately assessed until 1975, but since then the percentage lacking rudimentary skills has been reduced from 18 to 12 percent.

The percentage of students from at-risk minority groups who showed adept reading skills also increased across this time period, though the gap between their performance and that of their White age-mates remains quite large. In 1971, only 7 percent of the Black 17-year-olds read at the adept level, compared to 41 percent of the White students. By 1984, this had increased to 16 percent for Black 17-year-olds, in contrast to 45 percent for White students. Between 1975 and 1984 the percentage of Hispanic 17-year-olds reading at the adept level also increased, from 13 to 20 percent.

Changes in writing achievement have been less consistent and less encouraging. As was true of reading achievement, the difference in writing achievement between White and at-risk minority students seems to be diminishing at age 9. In recent assessments, White 9-year-olds showed mixed patterns of performance over time, whereas the performance of Hispanic 9-year-olds improved on all tasks analyzed in 1984. Black 9-year-olds also improved comparatively more than their White age-mates from 1974 to 1979, but did not continue to close the gap in the 1980s. At ages 13 and 17, however, the writing performance of Black and Hispanic students has remained consistently below that of White students, with no evidence that the difference is narrowing. In spite of the gains that have been made, there are still serious disparities in the educational attainment of these groups.

Children Without Home Support for Literacy

To what extent do children adopt the literacy practices of their homes?

The development of literacy is not solely a function of schooling. Some students live in communities and homes that foster literacy activities; others live in communities and homes where literacy activities occur less frequently.

Across a variety of assessments, for example, NAEP results consistently show that students from advantaged urban communities read and write far better than do those from disadvantaged urban communities. Similarly, the results show a consistent relationship between the educational environment of the home and literacy achievement. **Children and young adults whose parents have more education and those with access to more reading materials in the home read, write, and reason more proficiently than those from homes with less-well-educated parents and fewer reading materials.**

Figure 3.2 relates reading and writing performance to parents' level of education. The results are typical of those for such other measures as number of books in the home and variety of literacy activities. Children with home support for literacy tend to read and write more frequently for a wider variety of purposes, and this is reflected in their literacy skills.

Figure 3.2. **Average Reading and Writing Proficiency Levels by Level of Parental Education**

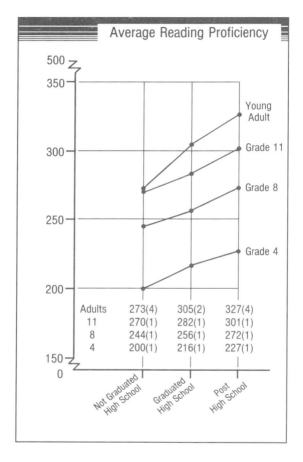

Average Reading Proficiency			
Adults	273(4)	305(2)	327(4)
11	270(1)	282(1)	301(1)
8	244(1)	256(1)	272(1)
4	200(1)	216(1)	227(1)

A Good Start in School

Preschool and the early elementary grades seem particularly important in setting the pattern of a student's academic career. A good start is self-reinforcing, providing a solid base of skills on which later achievement can continue to build.

The estimated population means are presented with their standard errors shown in parentheses. It can be said with 95 percent certainty that the mean reading or writing level of the population of interest is within the interval ±2 standard errors. Means and standard errors have been rounded.

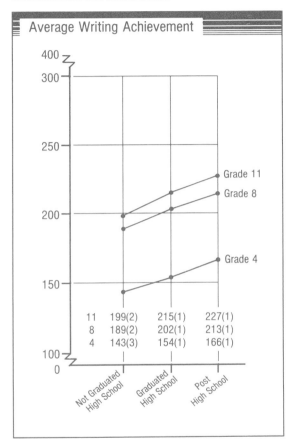

Average Writing Achievement

	Not Graduated High School	Graduated High School	Post High School
11	199(2)	215(1)	227(1)
8	189(2)	202(1)	213(1)
4	143(3)	154(1)	166(1)

NAEP reading data indicate that a good start in school may have contributed to the increased reading proficiency of minority students. Gains made by 9-year-olds in the 1970s (after the introduction of early intervention programs such as Head Start) were maintained when their birth cohorts were reassessed at ages 13 and 17. However, Black nine-year-olds in the most recent assessment showed no further improvement in reading skills relative to the previous assessment, and Hispanic children showed little if any improvement. This leveling off in performance could suggest that homes and schools are not providing enough early support to continue to close the gap in performance—and this gap remains large.

Conclusion

It is clear that in America, children from some groups are less likely to become literate than are children from others. Black children, Hispanic children, children living in disadvantaged urban communities, and those whose parents have low levels of education are at particular risk for future educational failure. Further, once these children begin their schooling at a disadvantage, they are unlikely to catch up. Black students appear to be in particular jeopardy, because as young adults they tend to have comparatively poorer literacy skills than do other groups. As a country we know these disparities exist and that they are detrimental to our society. It is time to ensure that these children get the good start they need; it is a crucial step toward eradicating unequal educational opportunities from our schools.

Chapter

The Effects of Instruction

Performance levels are interesting benchmarks, telling us how well we are doing—but they do not explain the causes of our successes and failures, nor do they help us understand what can be done to raise the level of literacy in America. Although NAEP data do not establish cause and effect, it is informative to examine the relationship between particular instructional emphases and achievement in reading and writing.

Instruction Does Matter

A variety of findings in recent assessments suggest that instruction does indeed make a difference. As we have already seen in Chapter 2, on average, reading and writing performance improves with amount of schooling. And, as reported in Chapter 3, groups of students who do well in the early grades are likely to continue to do well in later years. An early advantage may pay continuing dividends.

The national assessments of the performance of children in school have also examined a few general aspects of their educational experience, such as the amount of homework they have completed recently, the number of pages of reading they have done for school, and the number of writing assignments completed. Results for eleventh graders from the most recent assessments are summarized in **Figure 4.1. The findings indicate a consistent, positive relationship between the amount of schoolwork and achievement in both reading and writing.** (The lower achievement for large numbers of reports and essays reflects the performance of less able students who tend to be given a greater number of short, simple assignments.) Such findings are consistent with recent calls for increasing the emphasis on traditional academic studies, particularly at the high school

Figure 4.1 **Relationship Between Amount of Work for School at Grade 11 and Reading and Writing Proficiency**

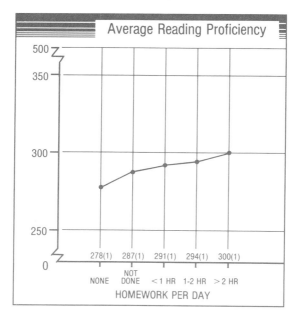

level. They make sense: Students who study harder are likely to become more literate than those who do not.

The Concern with Effective Reasoning

As educators and the general public have become more concerned with students' lack of ability to think critically about the materials they read and write, they have begun to encourage schools to focus more intensively on the development of effective reasoning skills. One manifestation of this concern has been a greater emphasis on what students do as they read and write;

The estimated population means are presented with their standard errors shown in parentheses. It can be said with 95 percent certainty that the mean reading or writing level of the population of interest is within the interval ± 2 standard errors. Means and standard errors have been rounded.

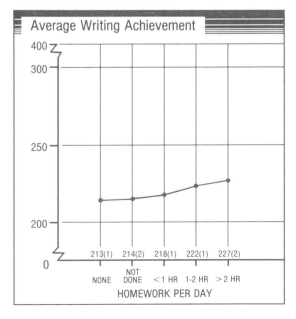

Average Writing Achievement

HOMEWORK PER DAY

NONE	NOT DONE	<1 HR	1-2 HR	>2 HR
213(1)	214(2)	218(1)	222(1)	227(2)

Figure 4.1 (Cont.) **Relationship Between Amount of Work for School at Grade 11 and Reading and Writing Proficiency**

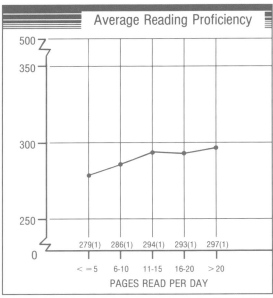

Average Reading Proficiency

	< = 5	6-10	11-15	16-20	> 20
	279(1)	286(1)	294(1)	293(1)	297(1)

PAGES READ PER DAY

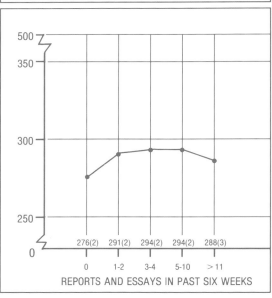

	0	1-2	3-4	5-10	> 11
	276(2)	291(2)	294(2)	294(2)	288(3)

REPORTS AND ESSAYS IN PAST SIX WEEKS

The estimated population means are presented with their standard errors shown in parentheses. It can be said with 95 percent certainty that the mean reading or writing level of the population of interest is within the interval ±2 standard errors. Means and standard errors have been rounded.

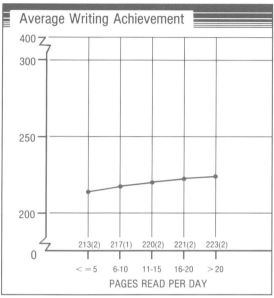

Average Writing Achievement

PAGES READ PER DAY

	< = 5	6-10	11-15	16-20	> 20
	213(2)	217(1)	220(2)	221(2)	223(2)

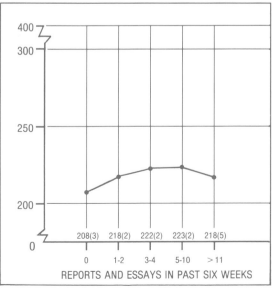

REPORTS AND ESSAYS IN PAST SIX WEEKS

	0	1-2	3-4	5-10	> 11
	208(3)	218(2)	222(2)	223(2)	218(5)

this is usually discussed as "process-oriented" instruction, since it focuses on the processes that occur over time as people read and write.

Process-oriented instruction in writing is usually considered a particularly useful way to develop effective reasoning skills, because writing requires focused attention and leaves a permanent record of the student's reasoning. In this context, teachers of English have been encouraged to spend more time on individual writing assignments, and teachers of other subjects have been asked to include writing activities as part of their curricula. These emphases have had some effect, in that time spent on writing instruction has increased. When students in 1974 were asked how much time they spent in English class on writing instruction, almost half (48 percent) of the 17-year-olds reported little or none. A decade later, only one third (35 percent) reported little or no time spent on writing instruction.

These changes in instruction may not have been as beneficial as had been hoped, however. NAEP's examination of changes in reading and writing performance across the 1970s and 1980s indicates that 9-, 13-, and 17-year-olds today are only slightly more literate than their predecessors. Trends in writing achievement between 1974 and 1984 show that, at best, performance in 1984 had recovered to earlier levels after some dropping off in the middle of the decade. Reading proficiency improved across time at all three ages, but these gains were concentrated at lower proficiency levels rather than reflecting substantial increases in the ability to reason effectively about what was being read.

Why have these instructional reforms had little effect?

To some extent the trends across time may reflect a general lack of attention to helping students reason effectively about what and how they are reading and writing. The decade of the 1970s in particular was an era of emphasis on the "basics," which often required only surface understanding. As assessment results indicate, schools have been quite successful in developing students' abilities to read and write at such a surface level. Yet the ability to understand at a surface level is only one component of literacy, and exclusive emphasis on the basics may be delaying attention to helping students develop effective reasoning skills.

Recent reform movements emphasizing the teaching of reasoning as part of literacy education (particularly as represented by the process approaches to reading and writing instruction) may have also gone somewhat astray. The 1984 assessment asked students a large number of questions about the instruction they had received and related their responses to their reading and writing achievement. Many of the relationships were encouraging: Higher achievement was associated with reading and writing more frequently, with more response from the teacher, and with *less* focus on the final product (when there is no opportunity to ponder and make use of the suggestions in thoughtful ways). Also, students who used process-oriented writing strategies—planning, revising, editing—wrote better.

However, a variety of teaching approaches that are specifically meant to encourage students to pay more attention to the process of reading and writing were less clearly related to achievement. Results for a scale based on a variety of aspects of process-oriented writing instruction are summarized in **Figure 4.2**. Students who reported their teachers emphasized process-oriented approaches (including teachers' suggestions to make notes before writing, get

Figure 4.2. **Average Writing Achievement for Students in Grades 4, 8, and 11 by Extent of Process-Oriented Teaching Activities**

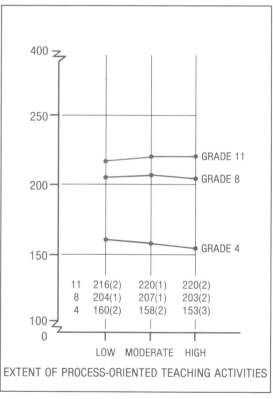

	LOW	MODERATE	HIGH
11	216(2)	220(1)	220(2)
8	204(1)	207(1)	203(2)
4	160(2)	158(2)	153(3)

EXTENT OF PROCESS-ORIENTED TEACHING ACTIVITIES

The estimated population means are presented with their standard errors shown in parentheses. It can be said with 95 percent certainty that the mean reading or writing level of the population of interest is within the interval ± 2 standard errors. Means and standard errors have been rounded.

responses from classmates while writing, and write multiple drafts) wrote no better than those who reported little or no process instruction.

There is no comparable scale available for the reading assessment, but results for individual questions were similar: Increased use of such teaching approaches as having students answer their own questions about what they read, take notes, and learn how to find the main idea of a paragraph were inconsistently and sometimes even negatively related to reading proficiency (**Figure 4.3**).

Such instructional activities have been at the heart of recent calls for reform in the teaching of reading and writing. That they are not positively related to achievement may suggest that although they have been used, they may have been discussed and implemented in a superficial way or primarily used with the weaker students who need extra attention.

At its best, instruction in reading and writing processes provides students with powerful strategies for thinking about what they are doing. However, if such activities have been incorporated into classrooms in ways divorced from actual reading and writing tasks, and without teaching students how to use them to advantage in their own reading and writing, the potential of such activities to improve student performance may have been unwittingly subverted.

Figure 4.3 **Relationships Between Use of Reading Process Activities and Reading Proficiency**

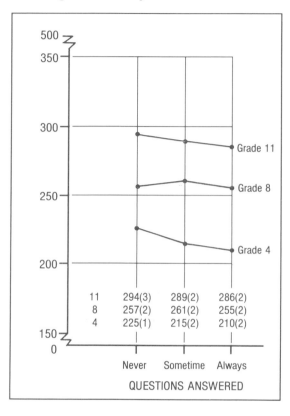

Simply providing students with exposure to new activities may not be enough to ensure they learn how to use these skills effectively for improving their reading, writing, and reasoning. Students may need to have more direct instruction about when and

The estimated population means are presented with their standard errors shown in parentheses. It can be said with 95 percent certainty that the mean reading or writing level of the population of interest is within the interval ±2 standard errors. Means and standard errors have been rounded.

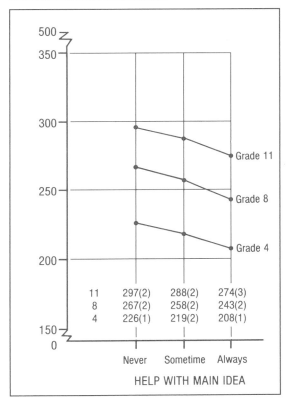

	Never	Sometime	Always
11	297(2)	288(2)	274(3)
8	267(2)	258(2)	243(2)
4	226(1)	219(2)	208(1)

HELP WITH MAIN IDEA

how to use such approaches, to have more practice in using them to solve problems in their own reading and writing, and to be evaluated in a manner that allows them to use the skills they develop.

Figure 4.3 (Cont.) **Relationships Between Use of Reading Process Activities and Reading Proficiency**

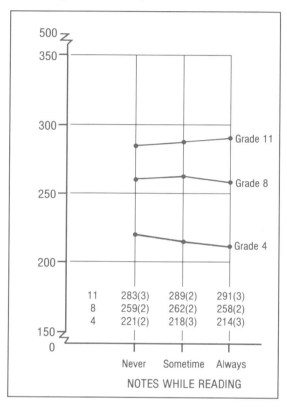

Conclusion

Schools do make a difference; an early start, appropriate instruction, and the emphasis on academic learning reflected in appropriate schoolwork and homework all contribute to young people's developing literacy skills. But schools do not and cannot work alone; home influences have a powerful effect on literacy achievement. Educa-

The estimated population means are presented with their standard errors shown in parentheses. It can be said with 95 percent certainty that the mean reading or writing level of the population of interest is within the interval ±2 standard errors. Means and standard errors have been rounded.

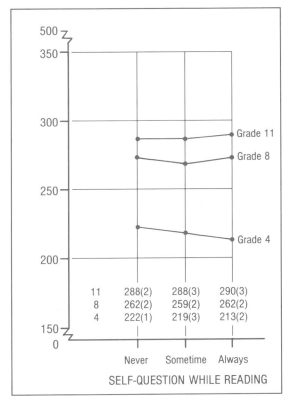

	Never	Sometime	Always
11	288(2)	288(3)	290(3)
8	262(2)	259(2)	262(2)
4	222(1)	219(3)	213(2)

SELF-QUESTION WHILE READING

tional reform movements that focus exclusively on changes in schooling and instruction may be limiting their own influence. The most successful programs may be those that include the home and community, involving adults in self-improvement as well as enlisting their support in the development of literacy in their children.

Chapter

Recommendations

Our examination of the development of literacy in America reveals both the successes and the failures of our schools and our society. On the one hand, the levels of literacy that have been attained by children and young adults are a remarkable national accomplishment in which we can all take pride. On the other hand, children are not learning the reasoning skills they need to meet some of the changing demands of our increasingly technological and complex society, and there are still major disparities in the educational attainment of various groups. We have done well, but it is crucial that we do better. Two important initiatives should concern us—as educators, as policymakers, and as a nation:

■ We must provide **targeted help** for the variety of at-risk populations to ensure that everyone has the opportunity to develop the varied literacy skills necessary for full and effective participation in our society.

■ We must modify our approaches so that more children will learn to **reason effectively** about what they read and write, giving them the thinking skills to analyze, elaborate upon, and extend the ideas with which they are dealing.

Achieving these goals will require systematic involvement from all levels of the political and educational system, as well as the development of creative alternatives to current approaches. To begin this process, we offer the following recommendations.

What Can Be Done...

...by Policymakers

Progress in addressing these two major concerns will require a redirection of resources and a redefinition of goals at local, state, and national levels. The following areas require explicit attention from policymakers:

Targeted Programs for At-Risk Populations. The disparities in performance discussed in this report are real and long-standing. Children of at-risk minorities and of the urban disadvantaged continue to be caught in a pattern of poor achievement that cannot be broken without more effective efforts at home and school. We have made progress in reducing inequities in the past, and can expect to continue to do so if we improve our efforts in the future.

Programs for Adults. The literacy practices of the home have a profound influence on children's achievement. There is an intergenerational effect on literacy; programs that are successful in improving the performance levels of adults will have payoffs in the achievement of their children as well. In contrast, ignoring adult performance may perpetuate a cycle of failure.

Academic Emphasis. The demands we make on schools should reinforce the academic goals of educational programs.

There is a temptation to ask schools to do too many things, many of which have little to do with developing academic skills. When priorities are set and resources allocated, academic goals should be among the top priorities.

Teacher Training. The problems we face in our schools cannot be solved simply by doing more of what we have done in the past. Solving these problems will require new initiatives and new approaches to teacher training, and the commitment to see them through. Universities, colleges of education, state departments of education, local districts, and schools should be encouraged to work together in addressing teacher-training needs.

Indicators of School Success. If our schools are to develop the advanced literacy skills needed by all of our children, we must use appropriate indicators in assessing their success. In examining literacy, we should use indicators that reflect students' ability to reason effectively about what they have read or written, rather than relying on measures of surface understanding. Assessments of writing achievement, for example, should examine students' ability to organize and express their ideas and should not be limited to their ability to spell or punctuate correctly. Similarly, assessments of reading proficiency should examine students' ability to explain and defend their judgments and interpretations.

...by Administrators

Administrators at the school and district level can institute change both directly and indirectly. They should support teachers who want to adopt instructional approaches and curriculum goals that will foster effective reasoning, and should take the lead in encouraging such initiatives.

■ **Supporting Instructional Improvement.** Administrators are the key to successful implementation of new instructional approaches. They can ensure that such efforts are systematic and coordinated, and can provide teachers with released time to plan, develop, and implement effective alternatives.

■ **Curriculum Objectives.** In addition to the facts that should be learned, curriculum goals need to focus on the ways in which new information is thought about and used. Administrators can encourage teachers of all subjects to adhere to curriculum objectives that focus on the ways students think about and use information when they read and write.

■ **Materials Selection.** Instructional materials and their accompanying tests should support student understanding beyond the surface level. Administrators can initiate a review in all subject areas of materials considered for adoption or currently used, to ensure they reflect these emphases.

■ **Community Involvement.** Local projects that bring parents into the schools and teachers into the community can change the literacy environments for at-risk children. Such initiatives can have a cumulative effect, improving the home environment for literacy and thus reaching children who have not yet begun school as well as those who already attend school.

...by Teachers

The results of NAEP assessments of literacy suggest that students need more practice in how to reason effectively in the course of their reading and writing. They need this practice with a wide variety of materials and for a wide range of purposes. This suggests a need for teachers to reexamine a number of aspects of their instructional programs.

Depth of Coverage. If students are to develop effective reasoning skills, they need to deal in depth with the materials they are reading and writing. Students need time to work on particular topics, and need thought-provoking questions from teachers and other students to help them as they refine and reformulate their initial understandings. It may be necessary to cover fewer topics, in order to provide time for students to explore particular topics in more depth.

Integration of Language and Literacy Activities. Emphases in reading, writing, and discussion should be consistent and should support and reward effective reasoning. Students need to learn to explain their ideas in ways that can readily be understood by others.

Variety of Literacy Experiences. Students need the opportunity to develop their skills in the context of a wide variety of literacy experiences. The differing levels of performance from task to task in the NAEP results reflect the fact that different tasks pose different problems and will lead to the development of different skills. Students need to learn to deal effectively with the full range of purposes for reading and writing.

■ **High Expectations.** Students are likely to benefit from a classroom environment where expectations are high and standards are rigorous. Casual attitudes toward homework and a de-emphasis of academic achievement are related to lower achievement. This is true for groups of children that do well in school as well as those that historically have been at risk for school failure.

Our success in reducing disparities in educational performance and in developing higher levels of literacy can influence the future of the nation as a whole. It can define the ability of our next generations to compete in the world economy, and may even affect the quality of life they enjoy within our own country. Our specific recommendations for change are not new, but they have never been implemented in a systematic and coordinated way. Without such actions many people will fail to develop the literacy skills they need and want for success in their work and daily lives.

THE NATION
REPORT
CARD